**CCSS** **Genre** Narrative Nonfiction

**Essential Question**
Why do we need government?

# A Day in the Senate
by Terry Miller Shannon

Chapter 1
Meet a Senator .................. 2

Chapter 2
Working Together .................. 6

Chapter 3
A Senate Vote .................. 10

Respond to Reading .................. 15

**PAIRED READ** A New President Takes Office ... 16

Glossary/Index .................. 19

Focus on Social Studies .................. 20

# Chapter 1
# MEET A SENATOR

Senators do important work. They make **legislation**, or laws, for our country. They pass laws to improve schools or build new highways.

Senators work in the **Senate**. The Senate and the **House of Representatives** make up Congress. Congress is the part of the government that makes the laws.

Laws help the country run well. Laws give us rules to follow.

Senators work in the **Capitol** building in Washington, D.C.

Candidates meet voters in their state. They want to win a seat in the Senate.

## Who Can Become a Senator?

A senator must be at least 30 years old. The senator must live in the state he or she represents. Senators make a **commitment** to serve for six years.

Senators also change laws so that they work better.

Voters choose senators to represent, or speak for, their state. There are two senators from each state in the Senate.

Let's look at a day in the Senate.

In the morning, senators meet with staffers. Staffers are people who work for senators.

Staffers do many jobs. Some find out information for senators. The Senate might be talking about a new highway. Staffers find out how much it will cost. They look at how the highway will change things for people living nearby.

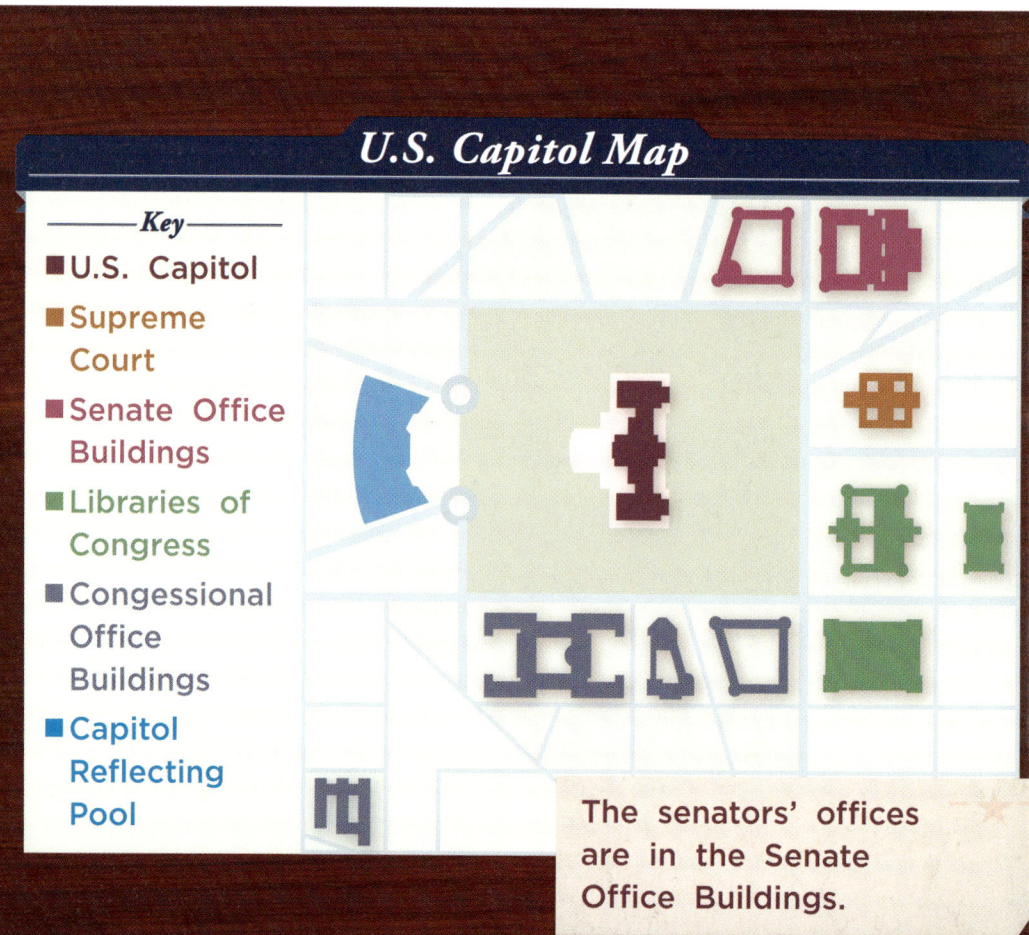

The senators' offices are in the Senate Office Buildings.

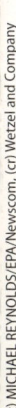

Senator Olympia Snowe of Maine (far left) meets with staffers.

Senators and staffers talk about the day ahead. Most senators go to **committee** meetings each day. A lot of work is done in these small groups.

Some committees study issues, or problems, that need solving in education. Others look at how the government spends money.

**STOP AND CHECK**

Why do we need laws?

5

# Chapter 2
# WORKING TOGETHER

After meeting with staffers, senators might go to a committee meeting next. Committee meetings take place in the Capitol building. Senators work on new **bills** at committee meetings. A bill is a law that Congress has not passed yet.

The education committee might talk about a bill about class sizes in schools. The bill would make class sizes smaller.

Senators ride the subway between the Capitol buildings.

People who agree with the bill say that students will read better in smaller classes. If Congress passes the bill, more teachers will be needed.

The committee wants more information. **Experts** who know how students learn to read talk to the committee. They say that smaller classes help students learn to read.

Next, the committee might add **amendments**, or changes, to the bill. Then it votes on whether to send the bill to the Senate.

The senators will talk about the bill.

Senators may eat lunch after a committee meeting. The Capitol and its buildings are like a small city. There are **cafeterias** and a gym.

Senators can eat in a cafeteria in the Capitol and its buildings.

**STOP AND CHECK**

What does a committee do?

# The History of the Capitol

This is a photo of the Capitol after the dome was taken down.

People began building the Capitol in 1793. The Senate wing was finished in 1800. British soldiers set fire to the Capitol during the War of 1812. The building was repaired. The Capitol was made larger in the 1850s.

In the 1850s, the dome was taken down. A new dome was built.

# Chapter 3
# A SENATE VOTE

Senators meet in the Senate Chamber after lunch. They talk about laws. They vote on bills.

Senators have the **privilege** of speech. This means they can speak freely in the **chamber**, or hall.

### Senate Pages

Senate pages are high school students who work in Congress. In the morning, they go to a school at the Senate. They work in the afternoon. The pages deliver messages and documents around the Capitol.

When senators vote on a bill, a person writes down each vote.

A bill is approved if it gets enough votes. Senators send their bills to the House of Representatives to vote on. Both houses must agree on the final bill.

The Senate and the House of Representatives sometimes can't agree on a bill. They work in a committee to figure out how to agree.

This page met President Obama.

People often change bills. This happens because people have different ideas. They need to **compromise**, or change their **views**. Then they agree on a final **version**.

A bill is sent to the president after the two houses agree on it. The bill becomes a law when the president signs it. The president can **refuse**, or decide not to, sign a bill.

People work together to get bills passed.

Visitors in the Senate Gallery watch the senators working.

Senators meet with people from their home state. People can ask the senators questions and share their ideas. Senators also meet with students that visit Congress.

Senators might fly home at the end of the day. At home, they meet with voters. The voters talk about their issues. The senators take those issues to Washington, D.C. **Eventually**, the issues may become law.

**STOP AND CHECK**

How does a bill become a law?

A senator meets with voters.

## Summarize

Summarize the work a senator does each day. Your graphic organizer may help you.

| Cause → Effect |
|---|
| → |
| → |
| → |
| → |

## Text Evidence

1. Reread page 7. What happens after a committee gets information about a bill? **CAUSE AND EFFECT**

2. Find the word *issues* on page 5. What does it mean? What clues helped you figure out the meaning? **VOCABULARY**

3. Write about how senators work with other people to make laws. **WRITE ABOUT READING**

**CCSS** Genre **Expository Text**

**Compare Texts**
Read about a new president's first day.

# A New President Takes Office

The United States is a **democracy**. This means the country is governed by the people. The president leads the country.

A president is elected every four years. The president officially becomes president on Inauguration Day. The inauguration takes place in front of the Capitol.

President Barack Obama became the president on January 20, 2009.

More than a million people go to the inauguration.

The new president takes the **oath** of office on Inauguration Day. The president promises to "preserve, protect and defend the Constitution of the United States." Then the president gives a speech.

Presidents talk about their goals in their speeches. Abraham Lincoln gave a speech in 1861. At that time, some states wanted to break away from the United States. President Lincoln said that he would work hard to keep the country together.

Abraham Lincoln takes the oath of office.

### Make Connections

Why is Inauguration Day held?
**ESSENTIAL QUESTION**

Compare the role of a senator in *A Day in the Senate* with the role of a president in *A New President Takes Office*. TEXT TO TEXT

# Glossary

**bills** *(bilz)* laws that Congress has not yet passed *(page 6)*

**committee** *(kuh-MI-tee)* a small group that considers a bill *(page 5)*

**House of Representatives** *(HOWS uhv re-pri-ZEN-tuh-tivz)* one house of Congress; works with the Senate to write and pass laws *(page 2)*

**oath** *(ohth)* a solemn promise *(page 17)*

**Senate** *(SE-nuht)* one house of Congress; works with the House of Representatives to write and pass laws *(page 2)*

# Index

Capitol, 2, 4, 6, 8, 9, 10, 16

Inauguration Day, 16, 17

Lincoln, Abraham, 18

Obama, Barack, 16

Senate pages, 10

staffers, 4, 5

# Focus on Social Studies

**Purpose** To find out why people run for public office

## Procedure

**Step 1** Work with a partner. Find out what school boards do. You can find this out online, or you can ask at the school office.

**Step 2** Imagine you are running for your school board. Brainstorm why you are running. What kinds of things do you want to do for the school?

**Step 3** Talk about your ideas with the group.